PRE

CHAOS

Richard Codor's
best political cartoons satirizing the
Trump presidency's lies, insults and
madness from 2016 to 2021,
with written historical context by
veteran reporter Roger Gnaw.

Loose Line Production, Inc.

For Sophia and Evie

President Chaos by Richard Codor
Copyright © 2024 by Loose Line Productions, Inc.

Edited by Tamara Glenny

Graphics by Ruhama Shaulsky

Research Assistance by Willa Pope Robbins

Design by Liora Codor

ISBN 978-0-9799218-4-1
First Edition, 2024

Loose Line Productions, Inc.

Published by
Loose Line Productions, Inc.

For orders contact
1-929-289-1990
richard@looselineproductions.com

Printed in the United States of America

Introduction

In the years before 2016, when Donald Trump was elected 45th President of the United States, he filed six separate bankruptcies for his companies, was involved in more than 4,000 legal disputes in various state and federal courts, participated in years of illegal tax write-offs, and conducted numerous affairs during each of his three marriages. Trump engaged in continual misogynistic behavior towards women, with one sexist rant even caught on tape. He frequently used racist language and tropes, claimed that Obama's American birth certificate was fake and never apologized for his 1989 call for the death penalty for the so-called Central Park Five for a crime they didn't commit. Trump and his campaign staff covertly and publicly engaged with Russian state agents with the aim of disrupting and interfering in the 2016 election.

And the list goes on.

Nevertheless, there were hopes that the responsibility and majesty of the office of the presidency would have an uplifting effect on Donald Trump's character and morals. Unfortunately for all of us, the reverse was true. As it turned out, the presidency amplified his bad behavior and brought out the worst in many of his followers, who have evolved into rabid supporters of a cult of personality.

I have been making cartoons about Trump for local and national publications since 1986. This collection highlights many of the events that we all lived through between September 2016 and February 2021. Each drawing is accompanied by a short, researched explanation and relevant quotations and tweets about the incident that inspired it. But while the cartoons may be humorous, absurd, or just plain goofy, the message is serious. For those who may have forgotten what things were like or believe that life was better during Trump's administration, I hope to show that that was not the case. It was a time of lies, insults, madness, and chaos. It divided our country and threatened the very essence of our democracy.

We can't be complacent. We mustn't let it happen again.

Richard Codor

October 4, 2016

Hillary Clinton campaigns on a large range of policies, including on the rights of women and minorities and highlighting her extensive qualifications and experience in government. She warns that Trump and his supporters will try to stack the Supreme Court and overturn the law guaranteeing a woman's right to choose.

Trump attacks her handling of her private emails. He openly calls for Russia to hack her computers and make the contents public. At his rallies he calls for Clinton's arrest and led chants of "Lock her up!" He calls her part of the "swamp" and the "deep state". He tacitly encourages white supremacist groups' support and prompts outrageous conspiracy theories suggesting, for example, that Clinton has been part of a secret pedophile ring.

Trump boasts about his success with women and business acumen but ignores requests that he release his tax records, something that every presidential candidate before him had done.

Clinton is still ahead of Trump in all the polls.

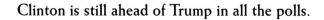

October 7, 2016

One month before the election, the *Washington Post* leaks a tape of Donald Trump's 2005 conversation with host Billy Bush on *Access Hollywood.*

"You know I'm automatically attracted to beautiful [women]- I just start kissing them. It's like a magnet. Just kiss. I don't even wait... And when you're a star they let you do it. Grab them by the p----. You can do anything."

Reacting to the leaks, Trump says, "This was locker room banter, a private conversation that took place many years ago. Bill Clinton has said far worse to me on the golf course - not even close. I apologize if anyone was offended."

Trump's apology: "I'm not proud of it. I apologize to my family. I apologize to the American people."

9

October 15, 2016

October 28, 2016

Just 11 days before the November 8 election, this news emerges in the *New York Times*:

"The Clinton campaign was rocked today when FBI director James B. Comey said Hillary Clinton's private emails were discovered on a computer belonging to Anthony Weiner, estranged husband of a top Clinton aide, who is being investigated for illicit text messages to a 15-year-old girl."

13

November 9, 2016

November 10, 2016

Election Day 2016 is over and Trump is the 45th President of the United States.

November 24, 2016

Trump's Thanksgiving video message to the nation:

"It's my prayer that on this Thanksgiving we begin to heal our divisions and move forward as one country strengthened by shared purpose and very, very common resolve."

December 9, 2016

While Trump waits to move into the White House, it costs $500,000 a day for nearly 200 police officers to protect his home of Trump Tower on Fifth Avenue in Manhattan, which also houses the Trump family business headquarters and will serve as the temporary home of the First Lady, Melania Trump, and the couple's son, Barron, for the early months of Trump's presidency.

December 31, 2016

In a New Year's Eve tweet addressed to the American people, Trump says:

"Happy New Year to all, including to my many enemies and those who have fought me and lost so badly they just don't know what to do. Love!"

January 4, 2017

Trump creates the role of chief strategist and senior counselor for Steve Bannon, CEO of the extreme right-wing website Breitbart News. He fires him seven months later.

"The President of the United States is a great man. You know I support him day in and day out," says Bannon.

One year later, Trump says, "Steve Bannon had nothing to do with me or my presidency. When he was fired he did not lose his job, he lost his mind."

January 11, 2017

President-elect Donald Trump holds his first news conference. According to PBS News, it is significant for his combative tone toward the press. He denies reports that Russia had obtained compromising personal and financial information about him. Referencing intelligence reports he has seen, he says, "I think it's a disgrace that information would be let out. I saw the information, I read the information outside of that meeting. It's all fake news, it's phony stuff, it didn't happen. It was gotten by opponents of ours."

23

January 20, 2017

Obama's Inauguration
2009

President Trump claims that his 2017 inauguration crowd is larger than Obama's was in 2009. Photos from the National Park Service and reports from many other sources show that his claim is wildly exaggerated. The estimates of Trump 's crowd size are in the 600,000-to-900,000 range, compared to Obama's 2009 crowd of 1.8 million.

Trump's Inauguration
2017

Trump directs White House press secretary Sean Spicer to say, "This was the largest audience ever to witness an inauguration, both in person and around the globe."
Senior Advisor Kellyanne Conway says, "That's why we feel compelled to go out and clear the air and put alternative facts out there."

January 26, 2017

Britain's Prime Minister, Theresa May, is the first foreign leader to meet President Trump in the White House. As she is on her way home, Trump signs an order banning citizens of seven majority-Muslim countries – including dual nationals from the U.K. – from entering the U.S. Mass protests erupt in both the U.K. and the U.S., and legal intervention stops the executive order.

27

February 13, 2017

Lieutenant General Michael Flynn resigns as National Security Advisor. He had misled White House officials about conversations he had with the Russian ambassador before Trump was sworn in as President. His tenure has lasted 26 days.

29

February 23, 2017

The Department of Homeland Security issues two memos that could expand the number of immigrants detained or deported from the U.S. In Trump's view, "We're getting gang members out, we're getting drug lords out. We're getting really bad dudes out of this country and at a rate that nobody's ever seen before."

March 3, 2017

Attorney General Jeff Sessions recuses himself from the investigation into Russian election meddling because he had twice met with the Russian ambassador during Trump's campaign, a fact that he failed to mention at his confirmation hearings.

At the Environmental Protection Agency, with coal miners looking on, Trump signs an executive order rolling back the Obama administration's Clean Power Plan, designed to cut carbon pollution from coal-fired plants. "C'mon, fellas, you know what this says?" says Trump. "You're going back to work!"

By the end of Trump's presidency, there are 5,000 fewer coal jobs, and coal-mining production has fallen by 25 percent.

May 25, 2017

Scott Pruitt, Administrator of the Environmental Protection Agency, says, "I think that measuring with precision human activity on the climate is something very challenging to do.... So no! I would not agree that it's a primary contributor to the global warming that we see."

Pruitt resigns in July 2018 while under 14 federal investigations.

EPA PROTECTED
-SCOTT PRUITT

CODOR 5/25/17 RICHARDCODOR.COM

June 1, 2017

"I was elected to represent the citizens of Pittsburgh, not Paris," says President Trump as he announces that the U.S. will withdraw from the Paris Climate Agreement.

"Coal is over," says Li Jun Feng, a renewable energy official in the Chinese government, four days later.

June 22, 2017

As the Republican-majority Senate unveils its proposed health-care bill, Trump's predecessor, former President Barack Obama, who succeeded in enacting Obamacare, the country's biggest expansion of medical insurance in decades, says:

"It is not a health-care bill.... It hands enormous tax cuts to the rich and to the drug and insurance industries, paid for by cutting health care for everybody else."

Senate majority leader Mitch McConnell says, "Obamacare is closing around us, and the American people are desperately searching for relief."

July 25, 2017

A sample of some of the highlights from Trump's speech to the annual Boy Scout Jamboree, held in West Virginia:

"Boy, you have a lot of people here. The press will say it's about 200 people."

"By the way, just a question, did President Obama ever come to a Jamboree?"

"Oh, you're a boy scout, but you know life. You know life, so look at you."

"And by the way, under the Trump administration, you'll be saying 'Merry Christmas' again when you go shopping. Believe me. Merry Christmas!"

"I know so many great people."

Z Z Z Z Z Z Z

July 28, 2017

After a seven-year quest by Senate Republicans to repeal Obamacare, the deciding no vote is cast by Republican Senator John McCain, soon after he is diagnosed with brain cancer.

In response, Trump tweets, "3 Republicans and 48 Democrats let the American people down. As I said from the beginning, let Obamacare implode, then deal. Watch!"

In 2024, more than 45 million people had health care coverage as a result of the Affordable Care Act and Medicaid expansion enacted under Obama.

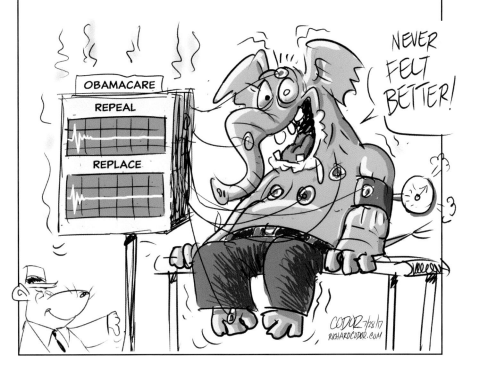

August 12, 2017

Violence erupts over the removal of a statue of the Civil War Confederate General Robert E. Lee in Charlottesville, Va. A "Unite the Right" rally includes armed white supremacists, Ku Klux Klan members and neo-Nazis in a torch-lit nighttime march, shouting "Jews will not replace us." The following day they clash with peaceful demonstrators, one of whom is killed by a car that deliberately crashes into the crowd.

On August 15, Trump comments to reporters, "You had some very bad people in that group, but you also had people that were very fine people, on both sides."

October 3, 2017

Approximately two weeks after Hurricane Maria devastates Puerto Rico, Trump arrives for a four-hour tour, visiting only Guaynabo, a wealthy suburb of San Juan. In a church he meets survivors, helps distribute supplies, and playfully tosses paper towels into the crowd.
At the time of his visit, 90 percent of the island's 3.5 million residents have no power or phone communications.
"There's a lot of love in this room," Trump says while giving out the supplies. "Great people."

Speaking to local government officials, Trump says, "Every death is a horror, but if you look at a real catastrophe like [Hurricane] Katrina, and you look at the tremendous, hundreds and hundreds and hundreds of people that died, and you look at what happened here, with really a storm that was just totally overpowering, nobody's ever seen anything like this."
He then asks the governor of Puerto Rico, Ricardo Rosello, "What is your death count as of this moment? Seventeen? Sixteen people certified, 16 people versus in the thousands."
The eventual official death toll in Puerto Rico was 2,975.

43

October 27, 2017

As special counsel Robert Mueller continues his investigation into possible Russian influence on the 2016 presidential election campaign, Paul Manafort, Trump's former campaign manager, and his partner Rick Gates are charged with receiving millions of dollars, which they laundered to hide the payments from the U.S. government, for their work on behalf of the pro-Kremlin political party in Ukraine. In the same month, George Papadopoulos, a former foreign affairs adviser to Trump, pleads guilty to lying to investigators about a Russian contact who told him that the Kremlin had Hillary Clinton's emails before they were released by Wikileaks.

December 22, 2017

Donald Trump signs the Tax Cuts and Jobs Act into law. It permanently reduces the corporate tax rate from a maximum of 35 percent to a 21 percent flat rate. Overall tax benefits for families with children remained roughly the same as they had been.

Trump tweets, "We are one step closer to delivering MASSIVE tax cuts for working families across America."

January 11, 2018

President Trump refers to Haiti and to some African nations as "shithole countries" during a meeting with a bipartisan group of senators at the White House. "Why do we need more Haitians? Take them out," he says.

January 30, 2018

At one hour and 30 minutes, Donald Trump's first State of the Union speech is the third longest in presidential history. While he calls for bipartisan unity to gather around him, no new policies are introduced.

"America is the place where anything can happen. America is the place where anyone can rise. And here, on this land, on this soil, on this continent, the most incredible dreams come true."

March 25, 2018

Stormy Daniels, an adult-film actress whose real name is Stephanie Clifford, gives a highly anticipated interview on CBS's *60 Minutes*.

Daniels details an alleged sexual encounter with Donald Trump, which she claims occurred in his hotel suite during a celebrity golf tournament at Lake Tahoe in 2006. She also reveals that in 2011 she was approached by a man who said, "Leave Trump alone. Forget the story," and threatened her life.

A week and a half before the election, Michael Cohen, Trump's personal attorney, paid Daniels $130,000 to suppress her story. After *60 Minutes* aired, the White House denies the story of the sexual encounter and the Trump Organization's involvement in paying hush money.

As this book was in production, Trump was in a New York City court facing criminal fraud charges in connection with the Stormy Daniels payment. He was found guilty by the jury on all 34 felony counts of falsifying business records in order to influence the outcome of an election.

May 3, 2018

Former New York City Mayor Rudolph W. Giuliani debuts as one of Trump's lawyers. At his first press conference, Giuliani reveals that Trump has been making secret payments to his personal lawyer, Michael Cohen, possibly in violation of the Ethics in Government Act of 1978. Everyone in the White House is caught off guard. A firestorm ensues.

May 7, 2018

Attorney General Jeff Sessions ramps up the administration's border policy, in hopes that detaining asylum seekers and separating children from their parents will deter immigrants considering crossing the border illegally. When lawmakers compare the policy with those of Nazi Germany, Sessions replies, "It's a real exaggeration. In Nazi Germany they were keeping the Jews from leaving the country, but this is a serious matter."

May 14, 2018

In a step widely seen as provocative and detrimental to the prospects for peace in the Middle East, the Trump administration officially moves the United States Embassy from Tel Aviv to Jerusalem. Israel's Prime Minister, Benjamin Netanyahu, and Trump's daughter Ivanka and son-in-law Jared Kushner, along with 800 dignitaries, relatives and friends, celebrate the move. Trump proclaims it "a long-overdue step to advance the peace process and work towards a lasting agreement."

Meanwhile, Israeli soldiers kill and wound Palestinian rioters on the Gaza border who are protesting the move.

May 16, 2018

The Senate Judiciary Committee releases emails and text messages relating to its investigation of a June 2016 meeting in Trump Tower between Trump's son Donald Trump, Jr., his son-in-law Jared Kushner, his campaign adviser Paul Manafort and a Russian lawyer, Natalia Veselnitskaya. The aim was to get dirt on Hillary Clinton and other political enemies of candidate Trump.

June 1, 2018

As part of his "America First" economic policy aimed at reducing the U.S. trade deficit by shifting from multilateral free-trade agreements to bilateral deals, Trump initially puts tariffs on solar panels and washing machines. He follows that on June 1 by extending tariffs on steel and aluminum to the European Union, Canada and Mexico, which retaliate in turn with their own tariffs. The trade war subsequently continues when he increases tariffs on China as well.

The trade deficit keeps going up.

June 4, 2018

In response to Robert Mueller's ongoing investigation into Russian interference in the 2016 election, Trump tweets:

"As has been stated by numerous legal scholars, I have the absolute right to PARDON myself, but why would I do that when I have done nothing wrong? In the meantime, the never ending Witch Hunt, led by 13 very Angry and Conflicted Democrats (& others) continues into the mid-terms!"

June 9, 2018

After the Quebec summit of the Group of Seven (Canada, France, Germany, Italy, Japan, the United Kingdom and the United States), Trump blows things up by refusing to sign the routine final communiqué. In a pair of tweets, he accuses Canada of imposing unfair tariffs and being a threat to America and insults Prime Minister Justin Trudeau as "very dishonest and weak."

He calls for restoring the G-8 by reinstating Russia, which had been expelled from the group in the wake of its forced annexation of Crimea from Ukraine in 2014.

June 26, 2018

In a 5-4 vote, with the four liberal justices dissenting,
the Supreme Court upholds Trump's travel ban from the
majority-Muslim countries Chad, Iran, Iraq, Libya, Syria and
Yemen, plus North Korea and Venezuela.

At the White House, the President tells reporters that the
ruling is "a tremendous victory for the American people....
We just need to know who's coming here."

July 6, 2018

Trump's Secretary of State, Mike Pompeo, makes a third visit to Pyongyang to negotiate North Korea's denuclearization. The trip is a total failure and nothing is agreed on.

Trump tweets, "If not for me, we would now be at War with North Korea!" and "There is no longer a Nuclear Threat from North Korea."

July 13, 2018

Before meeting Queen Elizabeth II, President Trump calls her "a tremendous woman."

Trump brakes royal protocol by being late to meet the Queen, shaking her hand instead of bowing, walking in front of her for the inspection of the guard and not knowing where to stand so that she must move around him.

The visit comes during Trump's tumultuous swing through Europe, during which he alienates NATO allies, sharply criticizes Britain's Prime Minister, Theresa May, and says that his upcoming meeting with Russian President Vladimir Putin might be the "easiest" of his trip.

After his visit with the Queen, Trump spends two days playing golf at his Scottish resort.

61

July 16, 2018

At their Helsinki meeting, Donald Trump, standing alongside Russia's President, Vladimir Putin, declines to endorse Trump's own government's assessment that Russia interfered in the 2016 election, saying that he doesn't "see any reason" why Russia might have been involved.

"I have great confidence in my intelligence people, but I will tell you that President Putin was extremely strong and powerful in his denial today," Trump says during a joint news conference, after he had gone against protocol and spent about two hours in a room alone with Putin save for a pair of interpreters.

October 6, 2018

Despite Dr. Christine Blasey Ford's testimony that he sexually assaulted her when they were both teenagers, Judge Brett M. Kavanaugh is confirmed to the Supreme Court by one of the smallest margins in the Court's history, creating a solid conservative majority in the Court.

Trump tells reporters, "Women, I feel, were in many ways stronger than the men in this fight. Women were outraged at what happened to Brett Kavanaugh. Outraged."

October 22, 2018

Speaking at a rally in Houston, TX, Trump says, "You know, they have a word - it's sort of become old-fashioned - it's called a 'nationalist.' And I say, really, we're not supposed to use that word. You know what I am? I'm a nationalist, okay? I'm a nationalist. Nationalist. Nothing wrong. Use that word. Use that word."

November 6, 2018

Due in large part to massive turnout by Democratic voters reacting to the actions of the Trump administration, the 2018 midterm elections give Democrats a net gain of 41 seats and control of the House of Representatives. About 10 million more votes are cast for Democrats than for Republicans, the largest raw-vote margin in history for a House midterm election.

November 14, 2018

In President Donald Trump's first year in office, the FBI reports that hate crimes increased 17 percent from 2016. In particular, there was a 37 percent increase nationwide in hate crimes targeting Jews.

November 22, 2018

Speaking with reporters and military personnel at his home in Mar-a-Lago, Trump says he authorizes the use of deadly force by 5,200 active-duty troops against a peaceful caravan of migrants who are approaching the Mexican-U.S. border, which he threatens to shut down altogether, while he claims that Mexico will "not be able to sell their cars into the United States."

The numbers of the caravan's migrants, mostly from Central American countries, dwindle as they travel through Mexico to the border. Many give up, return home or apply for asylum.

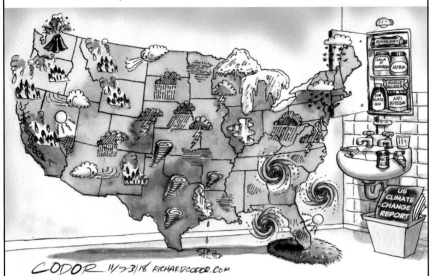

The Fourth National Climate Assessment, a major scientific report issued by 13 federal agencies, predicts that if significant steps aren't taken against global warming, America will lose 10 percent of its economy by the end of the century.

Speaking on *60 Minutes* on the subject of his climate-related policies, Trump says, "I think something's happening. Something's changing and it'll change back again. I don't think it's a hoax. I think there's probably a difference. But I don't know that it's manmade. I will say this: I don't want to give trillions and trillions of dollars. I don't want to lose millions and millions of jobs."

He later tweets, "Brutal and Extended Cold Blast could shatter ALL RECORDS – Whatever happened to Global Warming?"

January 25, 2019

ALTERNATE "STATE OF THE UNION" LOCATIONS

CODOR 1/25/19 RICHARDCODOR.COM

The 33-day shutdown of the U.S. government, the longest in the country's history, finally comes to an end. Trump and the Congress had been unable to agree on an appropriations bill, in which Trump wanted $5.7 billion for a border wall. Nine departments, employing around 800,000 people, were fully or partially closed and their workers furloughed. The Congressional Budget Office estimates that the cost to the nation was at least $11 billion.

Trump's State of the Union speech is delayed until the shutdown is over.

January 25, 2019

THE ADMIRABLE ROGER STONE

ENTERTAINING

GOOD FRIEND

HONEST

COOPERATIVE   HELPFUL   MUSICAL

CODOR 2/5/19 RICHARDCODOR.COM

Roger Stone, Republican operative, Trump mentor, and self-proclaimed "dirty trickster," is arrested in a pre-dawn FBI raid on charges lodged by special counsel Robert Mueller of obstruction, witness tampering and lying to Congress. He is eventually convicted on seven felony counts and sentenced to jail.

Stone's Rules

"Make your message big, bold and simple."
"Hang a name on your opponent."
"Attack, attack, attack – never defend."
"Nothing is on the level."
"Hate is a more powerful motivator than love."
"Admit nothing, deny everything."

On December 23, 2020, Trump pardons Stone, along with a number of his other associates.

Michael Cohen, Trump's former personal lawyer and fixer, testifies at a daylong hearing before the House Oversight and Reform Committee, saying that Trump lied to the public about business interests in Russia, lied to reporters about stolen Democratic emails and told Cohen to lie about hush-money payments to cover up sexual misconduct.

In his closing statement, Cohen says, "Given my experience working for Mr. Trump, I fear that if he loses the presidential election in 2020, there will never be a peaceful transition of power."

March 13, 2019

After numerous convictions and appeals, Paul Manafort, lobbyist, and former Trump campaign chairman, is finally sentenced to almost four years in prison for financial fraud uncovered by special counsel Robert Mueller as he investigated Manafort's alleged collusion with the Russian government in 2016.

Manafort gets 47 months. He could have been sentenced to 25 years. And in December 2020 he too is pardoned by Trump.

April 18, 2019

Attorney General William Barr holds a news conference to give his opinion on the Mueller report before it is made public. His version is the first volley in the Trump administration's campaign to limit the public's access to the full report.

"The special counsel confirmed that the Russian government sponsored efforts to illegally interfere with the 2016 presidential election but did not find that the Trump campaign or other Americans colluded in those schemes," he says.

May 8, 2019

Trump invokes executive privilege over the Mueller report, and the Justice Department refuses to release its full text.

New York Democratic Congressman Jerry Nadler, the chairman of the House Judiciary Committee, says that Barr has made the entire Justice Department an agency for enabling the President to defy the law, defy any type of accountability and act as a monarch.

May 30, 2019

Trump announces that he will impose a 5 percent tariff on all imports from Mexico, increasing to 10 percent on July 1, until "illegal migrants" stop coming to the U.S. through Mexico.

Beginning in 2018, the Trump administration imposes nearly $80 billion worth of new taxes on Americans by levying tariffs on thousands of products valued at approximately $360 billion. This amounts to one of the largest tax increases in decades, reducing real income in the U.S. as well as adversely affecting the country's GDP.

Numerous studies and analyses, including by the Congressional Budget Office, concluded that between Trump's inauguration in 2017 and March 2019, the U.S. trade deficit had risen to a level not seen since the Great Recession of 2008, while by 2020 average real household income had fallen by $1,200 annually.

July 15, 2019

CODOR 7/15/19 RICHARDCODOR.COM

In a tweet clearly directed at the members of the so-called Squad - Democratic Congresswomen Ilhan Omar of Minnesota, Alexandria Ocasio-Cortez of New York, Rashida Tlaib of Michigan, and Ayanna Pressley of Massachusetts - Trump says,

"So interesting to see 'Progressive' Democrat Congresswomen, who originally came from countries whose governments are a complete and total catastrophe, the worst, most corrupt and inept anywhere in the world now loudly and viciously telling the people of the United States, the greatest and most powerful Nation on earth, how our government is to be run. Why don't they go back and help fix the totally broken and crime-infested places from which they came."

All but Omar, whose family emigrated to the U.S. from Mogadishu in Somalia, were born in the United States. The tweet triggers the first official House rebuke of a president in more than a century.

August 7, 2019

A mass shooting on August 3 at a Walmart in El Paso, Texas, is one of the deadliest in U.S. history, leaving 22 people dead and an additional 26 injured. The 21-year-old white shooter was specifically targeting Latinos, as the anti-immigrant manifesto he posted online testifies, citing "a Hispanic invasion."

Four days later, Trump visits a hospital in El Paso where some of the victims are being treated. None will agree to meet with him. "This is a very sensitive time in their lives," says a spokesperson.

Trump and Melania also pose for photos with the newly orphaned child of Andre and Jordan Anchondo, who were both killed in the shooting. The President gives a thumbs-up while posing with the baby.

CODOR 8/13/19 RICHARDCODOR.COM

September 25, 2019

The White House releases a transcript of Trump's July phone call with Ukraine's President Volodymyr Zelenskyy, asking him to do a "favor" - investigating Joe Biden and his son Hunter for alleged dealings with a Ukrainian company. A whistleblower complaint citing concerns about the administration's attempts to bury records of the call is released the following day.

Trump tweets, "SUCH ATROCIOUS LIES BY THE RADICAL LEFT, DO NOTHING DEMOCRATS. THIS IS AN ASSAULT ON AMERICA, AND AN ASSAULT ON THE REPUBLICAN PARTY!!!!"

October 13, 2019

Trump abruptly orders 2,000 American troops out of Syria, without notifying our Kurdish allies or Congress. Believing that the withdrawal will end Western influence in Syria and hand full control to Russia and Iran, Defense Secretary Jim Mattis resigns.

Trump tweets, "We have defeated ISIS in Syria, my only reason for being there during the Trump Presidency."

The message from Russia's President Vladimir Putin: "On this, Donald is right. I agree with him."

Teenage environmental activist Greta Thunberg is named *Time's* Person of the Year.

Trump tweets, "So ridiculous. Greta must work on her Anger Management problem, then go to a good old-fashioned movie with a friend! Chill Greta, Chill!"

At the same time, a study published in *Nature* shows that the acceleration of ice loss in Greenland is reaching a tipping point expected to be a major contributor to global sea-level rise.

December 18, 2019

Donald Trump becomes the third president in U.S. history to be impeached by Congress. The House of Representatives adopts two articles of impeachment against him for abuse of power and obstruction of Congress. The inquiry finds that Trump withheld military aid and a White House meeting from Ukrainian President Volodymyr Zelenskyy, in order to pressure Ukraine into investigating Trump's political rival Joe Biden and to promote a discredited conspiracy theory that it was Ukraine, not Russia, that had interfered in the 2016 U.S. election.

Trump tweets, "The Greatest Witch Hunt in the history of our Country!" and "As I learn more and more each day, I am coming to the conclusion that what is taking place is not an impeachment, it is a COUP."

The United States Senate acquits President Donald Trump of his two impeachment charges. With the exception of Republican Senator Mitt Romney of Utah, who voted "guilty," the Senate votes along party lines and falls short of the two-thirds margin needed to remove Trump from power.

In his speech afterwards, Trump says, "I never thought a word would sound so good. It's called total acquittal. Total acquittal."

February 28, 2020

As reports increase from around the world of the potentially deadly effects of the newly named coronavirus, Trump suspends the entry into the United States of all non-U.S. citizens who have been in Iran in the past two weeks. This follows a similar proclamation made the month before, banning non-citizens traveling from China.

Previously, at a campaign event on February 10, Trump predicts, "Looks like by April, in theory when it gets a little warmer, it miraculously goes away."

On February 19, Trump tweets, "Highest Stock Market in History, By Far!" Five days later, he adds, "Stock Market starting to look very good to me!"

The stock market falls 1,387 points between the two tweets.

March 5, 2020

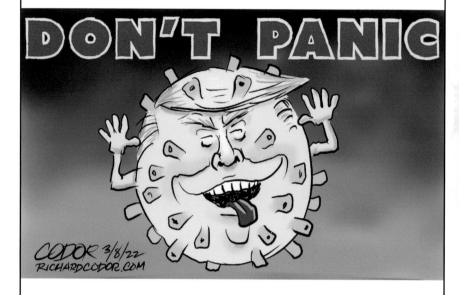

Trump meets with a Brazilian official who later tests positive for Covid-19. The President states that he is "not concerned at all." This comes as known cases in the U.S. have exceeded 500 and multiple states are declaring a state of emergency. Between March 4 and March 9 the *Grand Princess* cruise ship is forced to remain at sea owing to an outbreak of the disease among crew members and passengers.

"I don't need to have the numbers double because of one ship that wasn't our fault," Trump remarks on a visit to the Centers for Disease Control on March 6.

March 27, 2020

There are more confirmed cases of Covid-19 – over 100,000 – in the United States than anywhere else in the world, with the global numbers now above half a million. States such as California, Illinois and Oregon have begun to implement social distancing and stay-at-home measures in an attempt to quell the disease's spread.

A week later, Trump says, "I think wearing a face mask – as I greet presidents, prime ministers, dictators, kings, queens – I don't know, somehow I don't see it for myself."

April 1, 2020

At a coronavirus briefing, in response to a question about his tweets threatening Iran, Trump boasts that he is "number one on Facebook." He continues, "I thought that was very nice."

Facebook has no ranking system other than by numbers of followers, of which Trump has nowhere near the most.

The death toll in the U.S. from Covid has just surpassed 5,000 and the worldwide case total has hit 1 million. On top of that, the unemployment rate in the United States has now reached a high of 14.7 percent, with the largest one-month increase since data collection began.

During the daily White House coronavirus briefing, President Trump announces that he intends to cease funding the World Health Organization, the largest part of whose funding comes from the United States.

Trump tweets, "The W.H.O. really blew it. For some reason, funded largely by the United States, yet very China centric. We will be giving that a good look. Fortunately I rejected their advice on keeping our borders open to China early on. Why did they give us such a faulty recommendation?"

In fact, the WHO issued multiple warnings about the virus when it first took hold in China and is continuing to do so.

April 24, 2020

At the White House's daily Covid briefing, Trump suggests that ingesting bleach could cure the disease. "And then I see the disinfectant where it knocks it out in a minute – one minute – and is there a way we can do something like that by injection inside, or almost a cleaning? Because you see it gets in the lungs and it does a tremendous number on the lungs, so it would be interesting to check that."

Reckitt, which makes Lysol, tweets, "Under no circumstances should our disinfectant products be administered into the human body (through injection, ingestion or any other route)."

In an interview on Fox News, Trump says, "I learned a lot from Richard Nixon – don't fire people." He added, "Number one, he may have been guilty, and number two, he had tapes all over the place. I wasn't guilty. I did nothing wrong, and there are no tapes. But I wish there were tapes in my case."

May 29, 2020

A tweet by President Trump in response to the protests over the May 25 murder of George Floyd by Minneapolis police refers to the protesters as "thugs," adding, "when the looting starts, the shooting starts." The tweet is flagged with a label warning that it is an incitement to violence and Trump is banned from Twitter.

Trump responds, "Twitter is doing nothing about all of the lies & propaganda being put out by China or the Radical Left Democrat Party."

June 1, 2020

Police in Washington, D.C., use tear gas in Lafayette Square to forcefully clear Black Lives Matter demonstrators protesting about the death of George Floyd, so that Trump can walk from the White House to St. John's Church.

He is accompanied on the walk by staffers, Jared Kushner and Ivanka Trump, Attorney General Bill Barr, Defense Secretary Mark Esper, and General Mark Milley, chairman of the Joint Chiefs of Staff.

Trump holds up a bible, upside-down, for the photo op without uttering a word.

Trump's continuing use of the terms "China virus" and "Kung flu" has contributed to a serious spike in anti-Asian attacks both on social media and in real life.

Other minorities are also direct and indirect targets of the President. In a CBS News interview in which Trump is asked about the issue of Black Americans dying at the hands of law enforcement, he says, "And so are white people, so are white people. What a terrible question to ask. So are white people. More white people, by the way.
More white people."

August 13, 2020

President Trump acknowledges that he's starving the U.S. Postal Service of money to make it harder to process the expected surge in mail-in ballots, which he worries could cost him the election.

"If we don't make a deal, that means they don't get the money," Trump tells host Maria Bartiromo of Fox Business News. "That means they can't have universal mail-in voting, they just can't have it."

August 13, 2020

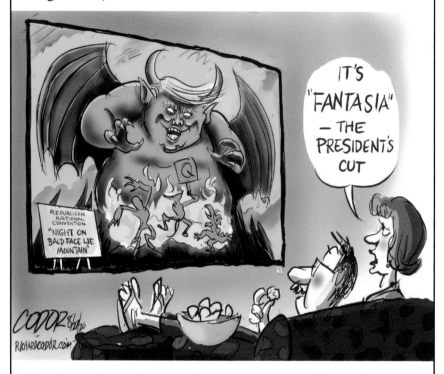

The Republican National Convention, much of which is conducted remotely owing to Covid-19 restrictions, culminates with President Trump's acceptance of the Republican nomination for president.

In his acceptance speech, Trump claims that if Joe Biden is elected, he will give "free rein to violent anarchists, agitators and criminals." He continues, "Joe Biden is not a savior of America's soul; he is the destroyer of America's jobs, and if given the chance he will be the destroyer of American greatness."

September 18, 2020

Less than two months before the election, Supreme Court Justice Ruth Bader Ginsburg dies after years of battling pancreatic cancer. During her illustrious career, Justice Ginsburg championed gender equality, reproductive rights and civil liberties. Days before her death at age 87, she tells her granddaughter, "My most fervent wish is that I will not be replaced until a new president is installed."

Immediately after her death Republican Senate majority leader Mitch McConnell begins the process of rushing through the nomination and confirmation of a new Justice, Amy Coney Barrett, before the election is held.

September 29, 2020

THINGS TO DO DURING THE NEXT DEBATE

BATHE THE CAT.

UNCLOG THE TOILET.

WATCH PAINT DRY.

CODOR 10/1/20
RICHARDCODOR.COM

BZzzzz

SELF ROOT CANAL.

At the first presidential debate, moderated by Chris Wallace of Fox News, Trump is out of control from the start. The debate is marred by insults, interruptions and shouting almost exclusively by Trump. Much of it sounds like his Twitter feed. Unable to get a word in edgewise, Joe Biden finally interrupts him with the line "Will you shut up, man?"

Trump continues his efforts from 2016 to undermine confidence in election integrity. Without any evidence, he claims that the election was already "rigged."

When Trump is asked to condemn violent white supremacist militias such as the Proud Boys, he replies, "Proud Boys – stand back and stand by."

November 7, 2020

Joe Biden and his vice-presidential candidate, Kamala Harris, win the 2020 United States presidential election with a total of 306 electoral votes and 51.3 percent of the national vote.

Trump refuses to concede, tweeting, "I WON THIS ELECTION, BY A LOT!"

November 19, 2020

Rudy Giuliani, former New York Mayor and personal lawyer to Trump, holds a news conference at the headquarters of the Republican National Committee in Washington. He harangues reporters with his baseless accusations of massive voter fraud. Forty minutes into his speech, an unidentified black substance starts dripping down the side of his heavily perspiring face. It appears that Giuliani might be melting.

Trump tweets, "I look forward to Mayor Giuliani spearheading the legal effort to defend OUR RIGHT to FREE and FAIR ELECTION!"

December 9, 2020

As Donald Trump and his allies continue to spread the claim that the presidential election was stolen from him – "the Big Lie" – the Supreme Court rejects a Republican challenge to the election results in Pennsylvania. Almost all of the 62 lawsuits contesting the election in various states are dismissed or dropped.

Trump tweets, "RIGGED ELECTION."

The people pardoned by Trump include close associates who were convicted as a result of the Mueller investigation in connection with Russian interference in the 2016 election – Paul Manafort, Roger Stone, George Papadopoulos and Michael Flynn. The rest include various financiers, lobbyists, party hacks and Trump's son-in-law Jared Kushner's father, Charles Kushner.

January 2, 2021

In a phone call to Georgia Secretary of State Brad Raffensperger, who records the call, Donald Trump seeks to overturn the results of the 2020 presidential election in the state, asking him to "find" 11,780 votes, one more than the margin by which he lost Georgia to Joe Biden.

January 6, 2021

Donald Trump holds a rally on the Ellipse in Washington, D.C., delivering a speech in which he encourages his supporters to march to the Capitol, where Congress is in session to hear Vice-President Mike Pence certify the results of the election. "We fight like hell," he says. "And if you don't fight like hell, you're not going to have a country anymore!"

After the speech ends and Trump returns to the White House, an armed insurrectionist mob storms and breaks into the Capitol, threatening to kill Pence, House majority leader Nancy Pelosi and anyone else they can get their hands on. One of the attackers is killed, while 140 police officers are injured defending the Capitol and guiding members of Congress to safety. Several police die afterwards, some by suicide.

Trump sits in the White House dining room for more than three hours watching the violent events at the Capitol unfold on TV while many aides and family members beg him to intervene.

Finally, at 4:17 p.m. he releases a video still claiming that he won the election and that there was massive fraud. In the end he says, "So go home. We love you. You're very special. You've seen what happens. You see the way others are treated that are so bad and so evil. I know how you feel, but go home, and go home in peace."

January 20, 2021

Joe Biden is sworn in on the steps of the Capitol as the 46th President of the United States.

Donald Trump ignores almost every tradition for outgoing presidents. He has not invited Biden to a meeting at the White House after Biden was declared the winner of the 2020 election. Outgoing First Lady Melania Trump has not invited Jill Biden to the customary tea and tour of the White House.

Trump does not greet Biden at the White House and ride down the Mall with him to the Capitol for the inauguration, nor does he attend the inauguration itself. He is the first outgoing president to refuse to do so since 1869.

February 13, 2021

Donald Trump, the only president or federal official to be impeached twice, is acquitted by the Senate in his second impeachment trial. Yet despite the controversy and the trial, he continues to dominate the Republican Party. Some Republican state parties censure senators who voted to convict Trump, reflecting their loyalty to him over traditional Republican principles. Over the course of the next four years, the Republican Party's fealty to its leader intensifies, to a point where it has truly become the party of Trump.

Notes

p.6   *The Washington Post*, Oct. 9, 2016, The deep disgust for Hillary Clinton that drives so many evangelicals to support Trump

NBC News, Oct. 4, 2016, Poll: Hillary Clinton Holds National Lead over Donald Trump

p.8   *The New York Times*, Oct. 7, 2016, transcript of the Trump sex tape

p.12   NPR, Oct. 28, 2016, FBI Led Back to Clinton Email Server Case by Anthony Weiner Investigation

The New York Times, Oct. 28, 2016, Emails in Anthony Weiner Inquiry Jolt Hillary Clinton's Campaign

p.18   President Trump video message, Nov. 24, 2016

p.19   *The Guardian*, Dec. 17, 2016, Cost of Trump family security vexes New York and Florida officials

p.20   @real Donald Trump. Dec. 31, 2016

p.21   ABC News, Jan. 5, 2018, Timeline of Trump and Bannon's turbulent relationship

p.22   *PBS News Hour*, Jan. 11, 2017, Watch: Donald Trump's first news conference as president-elect

pp.24-25 Vox, Jan. 24, 2017, A crowd scientist says Trump's inauguration attendance was average

CNN, Jan. 21, 2017, Comparing Donald Trump and Barack Obama's inaugural crowd sizes

p.26   NBC News, Jan. 26, 2017, UK Prime Minister Theresa May Applauds Trump, Urges Caution on Russia in Speech

p.28   CNN, Feb. 13, 2017, How Michael Flynn lost his job in 23 days

p.30   CBS News, Feb. 23, 2017, Trump says the new crackdown on undocumented immigrants is a "military operation"

p.32   *The New York Times*, Mar. 2, 2017, Jeff Sessions Recuses Himself from Russia Inquiry

p.34   *Politico*, Oct. 15, 2017, Trump's Love Affair with Coal

The Guardian, Mar. 26, 2017, Trump to sign executive order undoing Obama's clean power plan

p.35   *The New York Times*, Feb. 8, 2018, How to Read Between the Lines When Scott Pruitt Talks

p.36   Wikipedia, United States withdrawal from the Paris Agreement

The New York Times, Jun. 5, 2017, China Looks to Capitalize on Clean Energy as U.S. Retreats

p.37   *The Washington Post*, Jun. 19, 2017, Mitch McConnell on the health-care legislative process, 2010 vs. 2017

The New York Times, Jun. 22, 2017, Senate Health Care Bill Includes Deep Cuts to Medicaid

p.38   CNN, Jul. 24, 2017, The 29 most cringe-worthy lines from Donald Trump's hyper-political speech to the Boy Scouts

p.39   NBC News, Jul. 17, 2017, McConnell Pulls Plug on GOP Health Care Bill, Will Seek Obamacare Repeal

p.40   Wikipedia, Unite the Right rally

The Washington Post, May 8, 2020, The "very fine people" at Charlottesville: Who were they?

p.42   CNN, Oct. 3, 2017, Trump tosses paper towels into Puerto Rico crowd

BBC, Oct. 4, 2017, Puerto Rico: Trump paper towel-throwing "abominable"

p.44   *The New York Times*, Oct. 30, 2017, Former Trump Aides Charged as Prosecutors Reveal New Campaign Ties with Russia

p.46   *The New York Times*, Nov. 29, 2017, Trump Sells Tax Plan with False Claims

p.47   NBC News, Jan. 11, 2018, Trump referred to Haiti and African nations as "shithole" countries

p.48   ABC News, Jan. 30, 2018. Transcript: President Trump's 2018 State of the Union address

p.49   *The New York Times*, Mar. 25, 2018, Stormy Daniels Tells "60 Minutes" That Fear of Trump Kept Her Silent

Wikipedia, Stormy Daniels–Donald Trump scandal

CNN, Mar. 9, 2018, Michael Cohen says he used his own home equity line for Stormy Daniels payment

p.50   *The New York Times*, May 3, 2018, Giuliani May Have Exposed Trump to New Legal and Political Perils

p.51   CNN, Jun. 19, 2018, Sessions admits policy is a deterrent

p.52   Vox, May 16, 2018, The controversial US Jerusalem embassy opening, explained

p.53   NPR, May 16, 2018, What You Need to Know About the New Documents on the 2016 Trump Tower Meeting

p.54   Wikipedia, Trump tariffs
NPR, Mar. 8, 2018, Trump Formally Orders Tariffs on Steel, Aluminum Imports
p.56   CNN, Jun. 4,2018, Trump: "I have the absolute right to pardon myself"
@real Donald Trump, Jun. 4, 2018
p.57   *The New York Times*, Jun. 9, 2018, Trump Refuses to Sign G-7 Statement and Calls Trudeau "Weak"
p.58   *The New York Times*, Jun. 26, 2018, Trump's Travel Ban Is Upheld by Supreme Court
p.59   CBS News, Jul. 6, 2018, Pompeo says Pyongyang trip is "seeking to fill in some details" of agreement
p.60   *Politico*, Jul. 13, 2018, Trump meets with Queen Elizabeth II after calling her "an incredible woman"
p.62   CNN, Jul. 16, 2018, Trump sides with Putin over US intelligence
p.63   *The New York Times*, Oct. 6, 2018, Kavanaugh Is Sworn In After Close Confirmation Vote in Senate
p.64   *USA Today*, Oct. 24, 2018, "I am a nationalist": Trump's embrace of controversial label sparks uproar
p.66   CNN, Dec. 6, 2018, Latest House results confirm 2018 wasn't a Blue Wave. It was a blue tsunami
p.67   *The New York Times*, Nov. 13, 2018, Hate Crimes Increase for the Third Consecutive Year, F.B.I. Reports
p.68   CBS News, Nov. 16, 2018, Central American migrants streaming into Tijuana face long stay
CNN, Nov. 22, 2018, Trump says troops on US border can use "lethal force," threatens to close border
p.69   CBS News, Nov. 23, 2018, Al Gore says Trump administration seeks to "bury" climate report by releasing it on Black Friday
p.70   *The Washington Post*, Jan. 23, 2019, Pelosi tells Trump: No State of the Union address in the House until government is reopened
Politico, Jan. 23, 2019, "This is her prerogative": Trump gives in to Pelosi on State of the Union
Reuters, Jan. 25, 2019, Backing down, Trump agrees to end shutdown without border wall money
p.71   *Politico*, Jan. 25, 2019, Roger Stone's Last Dirty Trick
p.72   *Euronews*, Mar. 3, 2019, Michael Cohen gives damning testimony against US President Donald Trump
p.73   CNN, Mar. 8, 2019, Paul Manafort sentenced to 47 months in prison, far short of expectations
p.74   CNN, Apr. 20, 2019, 4 times Barr twisted and cherry-picked Mueller's report
p.75   CNN, May 8, 2019, Trump invokes executive privilege over Mueller report
p.76   *The Guardian*, May 31, 2019, Trump announces tariffs on Mexico until "immigration remedied"
Tax Foundation, July 7, 2023, Tracking the Economic Impact of U.S. Tariffs and Retaliatory Actions
The New York Times, May 14, 2019, Trump's Tariffs, Once Seen as Leverage, May Be Here to Stay
Politico, Feb. 5, 2021, America's trade gap soared under Trump, final figures show
p.77   *Mother Jones*, Jul. 14, 2019, Trump Tweets That Democratic Congresswomen of Color Aren't American
CNN, Jul. 14, 2019, Trump tweets racist attacks at progressive Democratic congresswomen
p.78   *The Texas Tribune*, Aug. 8, 2019, None of the eight patients being treated at the hospital Trump visited in El Paso wanted to meet with him
CNN, Aug. 9, 2019, Photo shows Melania Trump holding infant orphaned by El Paso killer.
p.80   CNN, Sept. 26, 2019, Whistleblower alleges White House coverup
Wikipedia, Trump–Ukraine scandal
p.81   *The Washington Post*, Dec. 20, 2018, Putin backs Trump's move to withdraw U.S. troops from Syria, says Islamic State dealt "serious blows"
The New York Times, Oct. 13, 2019, Trump Orders Withdrawal of U.S. Troops From Northern Syria

p.82   CNN, Dec. 13, 2019, We should all be appalled by Donald Trump's tweet about Greta Thunberg
The New York Times, Jan. 21, 2019, Greenland's Melting Ice Nears a "Tipping Point," Scientists Say

p.83   CNN, Dec. 19, 2019, Trump has been impeached, but he's still President. What's next?

p.84   *The New York Times*, Feb. 5, 2020, Trump Acquitted of Two Impeachment Charges
Politico, Feb. 6, 2020, In Near Party-Line Vote "It was all bulls—": Liberated Trump lets loose in victory speech after acquittal

p.85   *The Washington Post*, Feb. 28, 2020, Trump administration tries to play down the health and economic risks of the coronavirus
Al Jazeera, Feb. 29, 2020, US imposes new travel restrictions after first coronavirus death

p.86   *The New York Times*, Mar. 12, 2020, Trump and Pence Won't Be Tested After Meeting with Infected Brazilian Official

p.87   *The Washington Post*, Mar. 27, 2020, U.S. becomes first country to report 100,000 confirmed coronavirus cases
ABC News, Apr. 6, 2020, Trump, other top officials yet to don masks in public despite announcing CDC guidelines

p.88   *The Evening Standard*, Apr. 2, 2020, Donald Trump blasted on Twitter for boasting "Did you know I was number one on Facebook?" at coronavirus briefing
The Washington Post, May 8, 2020, U.S. unemployment rate soars to 14.7 percent, the worst since the Depression era
CNBC, Mar. 27, 2020, US coronavirus cases top 100,000, doubling in three days
CNN, Mar. 27, 2020, US has more known cases of coronavirus than any other country

p.89   *The New York Times*, Apr. 7, 2020, Trump Attacks W.H.O. Over Criticisms of U.S. Approach to Coronavirus

p.90   *The New York Times*, Apr. 24, 2020, Trump Muses About Light as Remedy, but Also Disinfectant, Which Is Dangerous

p.91   *USA Today*, May 8, 2020, Donald Trump said he "learned a lot" from Richard Nixon

p.92   CBS News, May 29, 2020, "When the looting starts, the shooting starts": Trump tweet flagged by Twitter for "glorifying violence"

p.93   *The New York Times*, May 1, 2021, Protesters Dispersed with Tear Gas So Trump Could Pose at Church
The Washington Post, Jun. 1, 2020, Inside the push to tear-gas protesters ahead of a Trump photo op

p.94   *The Washington Post*, Mar. 24, 2021, The link between anti-China sentiment in Washington and anti-Asian violence
CBS News, Jul. 15, 2020, Asked why Black Americans are killed by police, Trump responds, "So are white people"

p.95   AP, Aug. 13, 2020, Trump admits he's blocking postal cash to stop mail-in votes

p.96   CNN, Aug. 28, 2020, Transcript: Donald Trump's RNC speech

p.97   NPR, Sept. 18, 2020, Justice Ruth Bader Ginsburg, Champion of Gender Equality, Dies at age 87
Brookings, September 23, 2020, What impact will the death of Ruth Bader Ginsburg have on the 2020 Election?

p.98   *The New York Times*, Sept. 29, 2020, Chris Wallace Struggled to Rein In an Unruly Trump at First Debate

p.99   Wikipedia, 2020 United States presidential election

p.100   CNN, Nov. 19, 2020, Inside Rudy Giuliani's attempt to sow chaos on behalf of Trump and steal the election

p.101   PBS, Dec. 17, 2021, Exhaustive fact check finds little evidence of voter fraud, but 2020's "Big Lie" lives on

p.102   NPR, Dec. 23, 2020, Trump Pardons Roger Stone, Paul Manafort and Charles Kushner

p.103   *The New York Times*, Jan. 3, 2021, Trump, in Taped Call, Pressured Georgia Official to "Find" Votes to Overturn Election

p.104   Wikipedia, January 6 United States Capitol attack

p.106   *USA Today*, Jan. 20, 2021, Here are the customary things Trump did not do leading up to Biden's inauguration

p.107   Wikipedia, Second impeachment trial of Donald Trump
The Guardian, Feb. 13, 2021, Donald Trump acquitted in second impeachment trial

Acknowledgements

This book would not have been possible without all my friends who are committed to keeping our fragile democracy afloat.

Thank you to Tamara Glenny, who with a sharp editorial knife cut out hundreds of irrelevant cartoons and translated my garbled sentences into a readable text. Willa Robbins, my invaluable research assistant. Ruhama Shaulsky, who took the elements of our multi-layered design and graphically made it all fit.

As for our foremost enthusiastic supporters, Debra Solomon is right there at the top. Her advice, ideas and enthusiasm motivate us. Carl Silverman, equally enthusiastic, offered sage advice from a legal point of view. Moira Kelly for her inspiring activism. Micki Segel and Larry Sapadin, for their critical invaluable feedback. Shaun Mullen, my first newspaper editor, whose encouragement never wavered.

Finally, Liora, my wife, who designed the layout of the pages, kept the ship running and made sure I didn't slack off.